D1180665

# nickelodeon™

# SpongeBob
## SQUAREPANTS™

## This annual belongs to

Leo Edge

# EGMONT
*We bring stories to life*

First published in Great Britain 2013 by Egmont UK Limited
The Yellow Building, 1 Nicholas Road, London W11 4AN

Activities and story adaptations by Gemma Barder and Jude Exley.
Designed by Catherine Ellis.

© 2013 Viacom International Inc. All rights reserved.
Nickelodeon, SpongeBob SquarePants and all related titles, logos and characters are
trademarks of Viacom International Inc. Created by Stephen Hillenburg.

ISBN 978 1 4052 6762 5
54727/1.
Printed in Italy

No part of this publication may be reproduced, stored in a retrieval system,
or transmitted in any form or by any means, electronic, mechanical, photocopying,
recording or otherwise, without the prior permission of the publisher and copyright owner.

Stay safe online. Any website addresses listed in this book are correct at the time of going to print.
However, Egmont is not responsible for content hosted by third parties. Please be aware that online content
can be subject to change and websites can contain content that is unsuitable for children.
We advise that all children are supervised when using the internet.

Adult supervision is recommended when glue, paint, scissors and other sharp points are in use.

# Contents

A chance to win
£150 of book tokens!
See page 67 for details.

NATIONAL
BOOK
tokens

Here's **Spongebob StarPants** and his best friend **Patrick Sponge**. No, wait! Something is very wrong here! Colour in the two best friends while you work out what it is.

# Welcome to Bikini Bottom!

### 124 Conch Street:
## SpongeBob's Pineapple House

This is where SpongeBob comes to relax after a hard day's work at the Krusty Krab. It's full of modern conveniences, including a square toilet perfect for SpongeBob's ... erm ... shape, and a bed with three mattresses!

### 120 Conch Street:
## Patrick's Rock

Patrick likes things simple. Just like his house. Which is a rock ... and that's about it. But he CAN pick it up and carry it round with him, which is pretty cool.

### 122 Conch Street:
## Squidward's Tiki Head House

Squidward's house is a bit of mystery. No one's quite sure how the giant head got there, or why the equally giant-headed Squidward lives in it.

## Sandy's TreeDome

This is the one place in Bikini Bottom that YOU could actually visit! That's because Sandy's Dome has an air lock, which makes it possible for her to breathe underwater.

## Can you spot?

Many other oddball characters live in Bikini Bottom. Can you spot **Larry the Lobster**, **Barnacleboy** and the **Mayor of Bikini Bottom**?

THE KRUSTY KRAB

## The Krusty Krab

Owned by the money-loving Eugene H. Krabs, the Krusty Krab is THE place to be in Bikini Bottom. SpongeBob carries out his dream job here, cooking up delicious Krabby Patties from a super-secret recipe.

## The Chum Bucket (boo!)

Just over the road from the The Krusty Krab lies its wannabe arch rival, The Chum Bucket. No one ever goes here. EVER. It's disgusting!

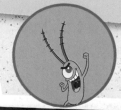

CHUM BUCKET

# The Tremendous Top 10!

## Top 10 facts every SpongeBob fan needs to know.

## SpongeBob SquarePants' Top 10 facts!

**Best Friend:** Patrick Star (and Gary, his pet snail!)

**Favourite Place:** The Krusty Krab – he'd live there if he could.

**Favourite Food:** Krabby Patties.

**Job:** Fry Cook (at the Krusty Krab, naturally)

**Favourite Colour:** Sponge yellow.

**Style:** Smart and square.

**Ambition:** To be Employee of the Month over, and over, and over again!

**Nemesis:** No one, really. He likes almost everyone (though not everyone feels the same about him!).

**Most Likely to Say:** "Time for work ... great!"

**High Point:** His hundreds of 'Employee of the Month' awards!

GARY

# Patrick Star's Top 10 facts!

**Best Friend:** Spongebob Squarepants.

**Favourite Place:** By SpongeBob's side. Preferably whilst jellyfishing, Patrick's favourite hobby!

**Favourite Food:** Anything. As long as it's edible, and even then . . .

**Job:** He's had a few, but likes his current position best of all . . . unemployed!

**Favourite Colour:** Lime green.

**Style:** Eye-catching swimwear.

**Birthday:** 17th August.

**Nemesis:** Anyone who's mean to SpongeBob.

**Alter Ego:** Patricia, his girly disguise!

**High Point:** Winning the 'Doing absolutely nothing longer than anyone else' award.

Patricia

**How many** jellyfish can you count on this page?

11

Answer on page 62

# Squidward Tentacles' Top 10 facts!

**Best Friend:** His clarinet

**Favourite Place:** His garden. Before SpongeBob's Pineapple House landed on it.

**Favourite Food:** Definitely NOT Krabby Patties. His tastes are WAY more refined.

**Job:** Cashier at the Krusty Krab.

**Favourite Colour:** Dishwater grey.

**Style:** Misery chic.

**Birthday:** 9th October.

**Nemesis:** Squilliam Fancyson III, Squidward's school friend and best enemy.

**Nicknames:** Bignose, Squidcakes, Old Man Squidward.

**High Point:** Having his house feature on the House Fancy TV show.

**Colour in** Squidward's musical instrument.

# Sandy Cheeks' Top 10 facts!

**Best Friend:** Sandy is friends with everyone, but she has a soft spot for SpongeBob.

**Favourite Place:** Other than the Treedome, Sandy loves her hometown of Texas.

**Favourite Food:** Nuts. She's a squirrel!

**Job:** A super-clever scientist and inventor.

**Favourite Colour:** Purple and pink.

**Style:** Oxygen suits and bikinis are the new black.

**Birthday:** 17th November.

**Nemesis:** She's not Plankton's biggest fan (but who is?).

**Alter Ego:** The Kung Fu master of Bikini Bottom.

**High point:** Winning the 8th Annual Goo Lagoon Anchor Toss.

# Eugene H Krabs' Top 10 facts!

**Best Friend:** Money.

**Favourite Place:** The bank, preferably looking at his money.

**Favourite Food:** If he could eat money, he would!

**Job:** Owner of the Krusty Krab.

**Favourite Colour:** Money green.

**Style:** Cheap. He'd never waste good money on clothes.

**Birthday:** 30th November.

**Nemesis:** Sheldon J Plankton of the Chum Bucket.

**Alter Ego:** Being a loving dad to Pearl.

**High Point:** The end of each day when he counts his takings.

## Sheldon J Plankton's Top 10 facts!

**Best Friend:** With all his plotting and scheming, he doesn't have time for friends! He even had to build his own robot wife, Karen!

**Favourite Place:** The Chum Bucket.

**Favourite Food:** Burgers, burgers, burgers.

**Job:** A crazed scientist and owner of the Chum Bucket.

**Favourite Colour:** Envy green.

**Style:** Genius meets madman.

**Most Likely to Say:** Darn you Krusty Krab!

**Nemesis:** Eugene J Krabs.

**Alter Ego:** He used to be Krabs' best friend!

**High Point:** Nearly discovering the secret recipe for Krabby Patties!

# Rock-a-bye Bivalve!

One of your Top 10 Fan Favourites episodes!

It was **just another ordinary day** in Bikini Bottom. Patrick and SpongeBob were waiting for the **newspaper** to arrive. They couldn't wait to play with the **rubber bands**, but something was **distracting them** from their play.

It was a **baby scallop!** "It's **totally helpless!**" said SpongeBob. "It looks like it **can't even fly** yet!"

"Y'now Patrick, since this scallop **doesn't have parents**, we should raise it ourselves," suggested SpongeBob. Patrick agreed. "**Just call me Daddy**," he said.

After a **hard day** looking after Junior, SpongeBob couldn't wait for Patrick to get home so **he could have a break**. "I'd love to help," said Patrick. "But I'm **totally wiped** from work."

Something told SpongeBob that Patrick's work **wasn't really work** at all. He was right! Patrick had just been hiding under his rock, **watching TV** all day long!

Patrick and SpongeBob got into a **huge fight**, until they spotted Junior **about to jump out of a window** – the baby scallop had learnt to fly!

"**Huh**," said Patrick. "That's all the thanks I get for **working so hard**?

The End

17

# Baby Love

## Check out these amazing baby sea creatures!

Baby **clown fish** are born and raised in an **anemone**, which is a plant that stings most other fish that tries to get in. Talk about **over protective** parents!

**Killer whale** babies are usually over **2.4 metres** long when they're born and weigh 180kgs! **Yikes!**

Baby **seahorses** are **tiny** when they are born (about 1cm long). They find other baby seahorses and **cling together** by their tails to keep safe. **Awww!**

As soon as a **Great White Shark** is born, it has to **swim away** from its mother as fast as it can, in case she thinks it's **prey** and tries to eat it!

**Sea turtle** babies aren't actually born in the sea. They hatch **out of eggs** buried on a beach and have to find their way **back to the ocean** as soon as they're born. Um ... thanks Mum!

A baby **grey whale** drinks enough **milk** to fill more than **2000 bottles** a day!

# Baby Stink!

**Pheee—ewww!** Babies might be cute but their *nappies stink!* Colour in this picture of Spongebob holding a bag of Junior's used nappies. Try not to breathe in the smell! *Ick!*

# MuscleBob BuffPants!

One of your Top 10 Fan Favourites episodes!

### Sandy says:

"SpongeBob's always been weak as a **newborn buffalo**, so I was really surprised when I visited his house and he told me he'd been **working out**. Thing is, his 'weights' were a bit wimpy. I mean, y'all can't build muscles like mine lifting teddy bears! So I did the only thing a true friend would, and showed him how I work out. He weren't too pleased about it neither, and soon he disappeared faster than a **barefoot jack rabbit** in hunting season.

Next thing I know, SpongeBob is down at the **Juice Bar** showing off muscles bigger than a haystack in August! They were incredible! So incredible that I signed him up to the **Annual Goo Lagoon Anchor Toss** competition that afternoon.

I was in first place when SpongeBob took his turn and I totally thought he would beat my throw. He stepped up to the anchor, **strained** and **squeezed** and whattaya know? His doggone arms **popped**! The big cheater didn't have real muscles at all!"

### SpongeBob says:

"I decided it was about time **I got big** and I knew just how to do it, too. Everything was going swimmingly and then my friend Sandy came over for a visit. For some reason she didn't think I could build my muscles using my **state-of-the art equipment**, so she showed me how SHE works out. She calls it working out, and I know she meant well, but, well, it was **torture**! I didn't really feel like seeing what **instrument of evil** she was going to use next, so I ran home.

I was just about to give up on my dream of having arms **bigger than a whale's behind**, when I spotted an advert for **inflatable arms**! Instant muscles!

Soon it was time to show off my **new physique** down at muscle beach. Then Sandy turned up again. She only went and **signed me up** for the Annual Goo Lagoon Anchor Toss!

All I could do was try my hardest, but my hardest try made my new inflatable arms **explode**! Oops. Sandy was **pretty mad**, but at least she won the Anchor Toss!"

# SpongeBob SwapArms!

## Now you can make **SpongeBob's dreams** come true and give him bigger and better arms!

1. Cut out SpongeBob and all the arms, below. If you'd rather not cut up your book, you can photocopy or trace over the page instead.

2. Push a split pin through the holes at the top of each arm piece, then through the holes on SpongeBob's sides.

3. Open the split pins out to move SpongeBob's new arms!

Ask an adult to help you when using scissors.

Squidward's Arms

© 2013 Viacom

© 2013 Viacom

Patrick's Arms

© 2013 Viacom

© 2013 Viacom

MuscleBob's Arms

© 2013 Viacom

© 2013 Viacom

© 2013 Viacom

# Sink or Swim?

SpongeBob needs something **heavy** to train with. All of these items will either **sink or float** when dropped into water. Choose which ones you think will **sink!**

| Plastic bottle | |
|---|---|
| Sink | |
| Float | ✓ |

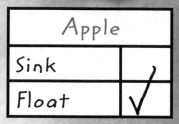

| Apple | |
|---|---|
| Sink | |
| Float | ✓ |

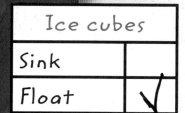

| Ice cubes | |
|---|---|
| Sink | |
| Float | ✓ |

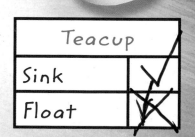

| Teacup | |
|---|---|
| Sink | ✓ |
| Float | ✗ |

Don't try this one out at home!

| Bunch of keys | |
|---|---|
| Sink | ✓ |
| Float | |

| Mobile phone | |
|---|---|
| Sink | ✓ |
| Float | |

**How many did you get right?**

**0-3** You've sunk faster than one of Mr Krabs' sacks full of money.

**4-6** You're floating in a big bubble of success!

Answers on page 62.

# Spot the Difference!

SpongeBob **LOVES** his driving lessons with **Mrs Puff!**
Can you find the **five** differences in **picture 2**?
Colour in a **jellyfish** when you find each one.

Answer on page 62.

# Sandy's Duck and Dive Game!

Sandy's been back to her **rootin'**, **tootin'** homeland of Texas for a **holiday**, but now she's back under the waves again. Grab a friend and **be the first** to get Sandy to her **Treedome home!**

**Start**

**1** Hitch a ride on a giant turtle. Zoom on 3 spaces.

**2** Clams block your way. Miss a go.

**11**

**12** Swap places with the player closest to you. Just because.

**13** Kung-fu kick your way forward 2 spaces.

**14** Larry challenges you to an arm-wrestle. Go forward 3 spaces when you wupp his behind!

**15**

**16**

**17**

**18** Stop to lasso an out of control jellyfish. Miss a turn.

**19** You spy a species of seaweed you haven't examined yet. Miss a turn as you find out all about it.

**20**

24

**What to do:**
Take turns to roll a dice and race around the board with your counters (coins or buttons will do), moving forwards or backwards as you are told! The first player to reach the TreeDome wins!

**3**

**4**

**5** Roll again, SpongeBob's getting bored waiting for you.

**6** You overhear someone talking trash about Texas. Go back 2 spaces to set them straight!

**7**

**10** Oh, no! You smelt an octopus' burp! Quick, float back 2 spaces!

**9** Feeling hungry? Go back 2 spaces and fry a Krabby Patty!

**8**

**21**

**22**

**Finish**
Yee-ha, you win!

# 20,000 Patties Under the Sea!

Add **any words you like** to this
Bikini Bottom adventure!

Based on one of your Top 10 Fan Favourites episodes!

One day, SpongeBob and Patrick were playing _____ when they discovered a submarine **buried in the sand!**

They clambered inside and found _____ .

"This is **great!**" said SpongeBob. He found the _____ and started the submarine.

Meanwhile, Mr Krabs was trying to find a new way to **make more money** when there was a loud _____ .

Spongebob and Patrick **crashed** through the Krusty Krab's window in their submarine. "That's it!" said Krabs. "You can sell Krabby Patties in this!"

SpongeBob and Patrick were having a really _____ time selling the Krabby Patties until they **fell down** a huge _____ ! Down there, they met a **giant, green sea monster** that looked just like _____ .

26

At first they were **scared**, until they realised the monster was just hungry, so they cooked up a whole batch of _____ . The monster was **so happy** that he kept paying SpongeBob and Patrick until he felt completely full.

Back at the Krusty Krab, Squidward and Krabs were waiting for SpongeBob and Patrick to return. Just then, the submarine crashed through the _____ . But Krabs didn't care, he just wanted to know **how much money** they had made. "Oh lots!" said SpongeBob. "But we had to lose some weight to drive out of the _____ so we **dumped it all**. We did bring back lots of shiny _____ though!"

**The End**

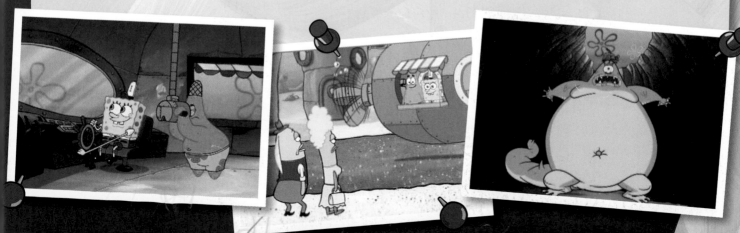

# How Many Krabby Patties?

Can you count the **number of Krabby Patties** on this page (including two **mega** ones)?

Wait a minute... there's a **microscopic menace** around! Can you spot **Plankton** trying to steal the Krabby Patty recipe for himself?

28

There are 16 Krabby patties.

Answers on page 62.

# Krusty Wordsearch

Feeling hungry? Sink your teeth into this **giant wordsearch** and find all these **Krusty Krab-themed words!**

| | | | | | | | | | | | | | | | | |
|---|---|---|---|---|---|---|---|---|---|---|---|---|---|---|---|---|
| T | S | R | O | Q | T | A | R | Y | P | L | O | R | K | J |
| A | P | L | A | T | E | S | U | A | Q | M | E | N | U | T |
| B | O | Y | G | I | C | H | A | I | R | S | E | L | Y | V |
| L | N | E | K | N | U | X | E | O | G | L | W | D | Z | S |
| E | G | K | R | U | S | T | Y | K | R | A | B | O | E | Q |
| S | E | B | I | S | T | V | A | E | O | C | T | K | H | U |
| E | B | R | N | L | O | D | O | O | F | L | A | I | S | I |
| H | O | E | L | N | M | E | K | B | T | H | V | Q | M | D |
| L | B | P | V | H | E | L | M | T | S | A | N | D | O | W |
| U | R | O | A | P | R | O | L | K | D | J | B | E | N | A |
| N | F | R | I | E | S | T | L | A | E | I | F | A | E | R |
| C | Y | D | E | D | N | I | H | Y | L | E | N | B | Y | D |
| H | R | E | U | C | M | E | D | V | N | O | R | N | I | S |
| T | I | R | M | A | E | R | C | E | C | I | F | Y | E | L |
| A | D | O | S | O | N | D | M | R | K | R | A | B | S | R |

CHAIRS     KRUSTY KRABS     PLATES

CUSTOMERS     ~~LUNCH~~     SODA

DINNER     MENU     ~~SPONGEBOB~~

FOOD     MILKSHAKES     SQUIDWARD

FRIES     MONEY     TABLES

ICE CREAM     MR KRABS

KRABBY PATTIES     ORDER

One of these words is missing from the wordsearch. Which one is it?

**29**

Answers on page 62.

# Form an orderly queue ...

FIRSE

DSAO

PASTIET

MHLKISKAE

**Unscramble these words** to discover what SpongeBob and Patrick are **selling from the submarine!**

Answers on page 62.

## Argh!

Draw the **terrible monster** coming out of the cave ready to devour SpongeBob and Patrick's Patties!

# Underwater Wordgrid

Can you fit all these watery words into the grid?
The first one has been done for you!

**Four letter words:**
Fish
Crab

**Five letter words:**
Shark
Coral

**Six-letter words:**
Bubble
Anchor

**Seven letters:**
Seaweed
Dolphin
Octopus

**Nine letters:**
Shipwreck

Shipwreck

# Big Sister Sam

One of your Top 10 Fan Favourites episodes!

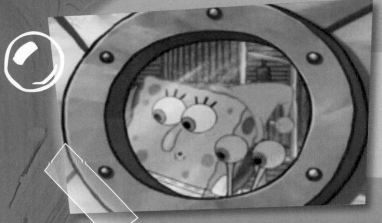

One morning, SpongeBob looked out of his window to see Patrick busy cleaning his rock. "My **big sister's coming to visit!**" Patrick said, excited.

Just then, a bus pulled up and out stepped Sam, Patrick's **BIG** sister.

Patrick and Sam were **really happy** to see each other. Sam decided the best way for them to spend their time was to make Patrick a **new house**, as his old one was **boring**.

Unfortunately, a small side effect was that **Squidward's house** ended up covered in sand! He wasn't happy. In fact **he was mad**, very mad and decided to come and give Patrick and Sam a piece of his rather large mind.

Unfortunately for Squidward, Sam wasn't going to let anyone **be mean** to her little brother, so as well as spraying sand all over Squidward's house, **she destroyed it, too!**

**SpongeBob** tried to make things better between Sam and Squidward, but ended up **face down in the sand** for his troubles. **Urgh!**

In the end, with most of the houses on Conch Street **destroyed**, it was finally time to say goodbye to Sam – she was **late for a manicure**.

"**Isn't my sister something?**" sighed Patrick.

"You **can say that again**," grumbled SpongeBob.

**The End**

**Now try the quiz about the story on page 34!**

# Quick-fire Quiz!

What's the **name** of Patrick's sister?

What was she **wearing**?

How was her **hair** tied?

Why did she want to make Patrick a **new house**?

What **did she do** to Squidward's house?

Why did she have **to leave**?

Answers on page 62.

## SpongeBob Funnies!

Did you hear about the boy who saw a witch riding on a broomstick?
He asked, 'What are you doing on that?'
She replied, 'My sister's got the vacuum cleaner.'

**Ha! Ha!**

Father: Why did you put a toad in your sister's bed?
Son: I couldn't find a spider.

**Hee!**

**Ho! Ho!** Brother: That planet up there is Mars.
Sister: Then that other one must be Pa's.

Sister: Mom wants you to come in and help fix dinner.
Brother: Why? Is it broken?

**Ha!**

Do robots have sisters? Yes! Transistors!

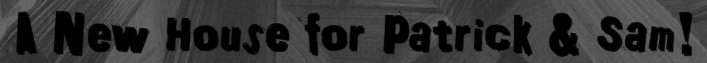

# A New House for Patrick & Sam!

Sam thought Patrick's house was **boring**.
Use this space to create a brand-new house for them!

Remember, Patrick is pretty lazy so the house should be low maintenance.

Leave enough space for a HUGE fridge.

An area purely for lying down is a must!

# What's Your Perfect Sea Pet?

Do you mind a mess?

YES

NO

Like things noisy?

Good at handling a bad temper?

YES

NO

Always up for some fun?

NO

YES

NO

Love running around?

YES

YES

Are you a scaredy cat?

YES

YES

NO

NO

Need a good pal?

MAYBE

YES

NO

YES

NO

### Bubble buddy!

Your perfect sea pet is a quite, hushed, silent bubble. Sure, he's shiny and you can do your hair in his reflection, but he can be a bit, well, BORING!

### Gary

Just like SpongeBob you and Gary would make perfect companions. He'd always be there to listen to your troubles as long as you polish his shell.

### Acid-spitting worms

You like a challenge, don't you! You're not afraid of anything and you don't mind if things get messy. These crazy invertebrates are just right for you!

# Consequences!

**Ever wanted to create your own crazy SpongeBob episode? Now you can!**

1. Pull out this page (or copy it onto a piece of paper).

2. Take turns with a friend (or two) to finish off the headings.

3. Once you have written your part of the story, fold along the dotted lines and pass it on to the next person.

4. When all the headings have been filled in , read out your story!

It was just an ordinary day in Bikini Bottom when ...

FOLD HERE

Just then, Sandy's Treedome sprang a leak, so ...

FOLD HERE

They couldn't believe it when ...

FOLD HERE

There was nothing else for it, Spongebob ...

FOLD HERE

So in the end they ...

NOW OPEN UP THE PAPER AND READ YOUR STORY OUT LOUD!

# Toy Store of Doom

Patrick and SpongeBob were bored. **BORED!** Even hanging out in Squidward's house **without his permission** couldn't cheer them up.

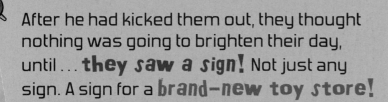

After he had kicked them out, they thought nothing was going to brighten their day, until... **they saw a sign!** Not just any sign. A sign for a **brand-new toy store!**

They ran and ran until they found the **Toy Barrel** – a packed toy store of which the likes had never been seen in Bikini Bottom.

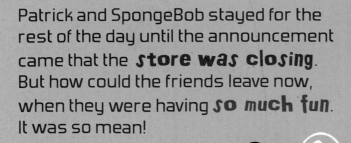

Patrick and SpongeBob stayed for the rest of the day until the announcement came that the **store was closing**. But how could the friends leave now, when they were having **so much fun**. It was so mean!

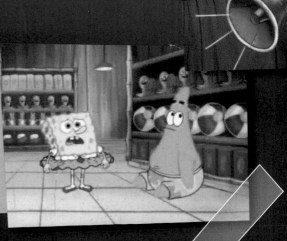

Luckily, SpongeBob **had a plan!** He and Patrick hid in a doll's house until the coast was clear, then the store was **all theirs!**

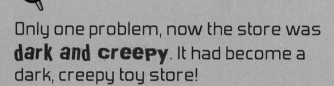

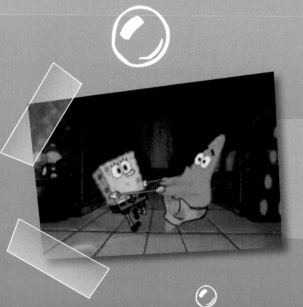

Only one problem, now the store was **dark and creepy**. It had become a dark, creepy toy store!

There was only one thing for it. They had to arm themselves . . . **with bubbles!**

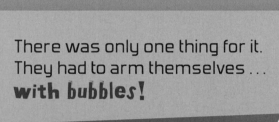

Somehow they made it through the night and were released into the warm light of day. With their **new-found freedom** there was only one thing left to do.

**Go back** to the toy store!

**The End**

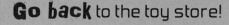

# Toydoku!

SpongeBob and Patrick **LOVE** their toys! Can you place **each toy only once** in each column, row and square? You can use the key instead of drawing the toys if you like e.g. Teddy = **1**

● All 6 toys appear once in each row **across** →
● All 6 toys appear once in each row **down** ↓
● All 6 toys appear once in each **set of 6 boxes**

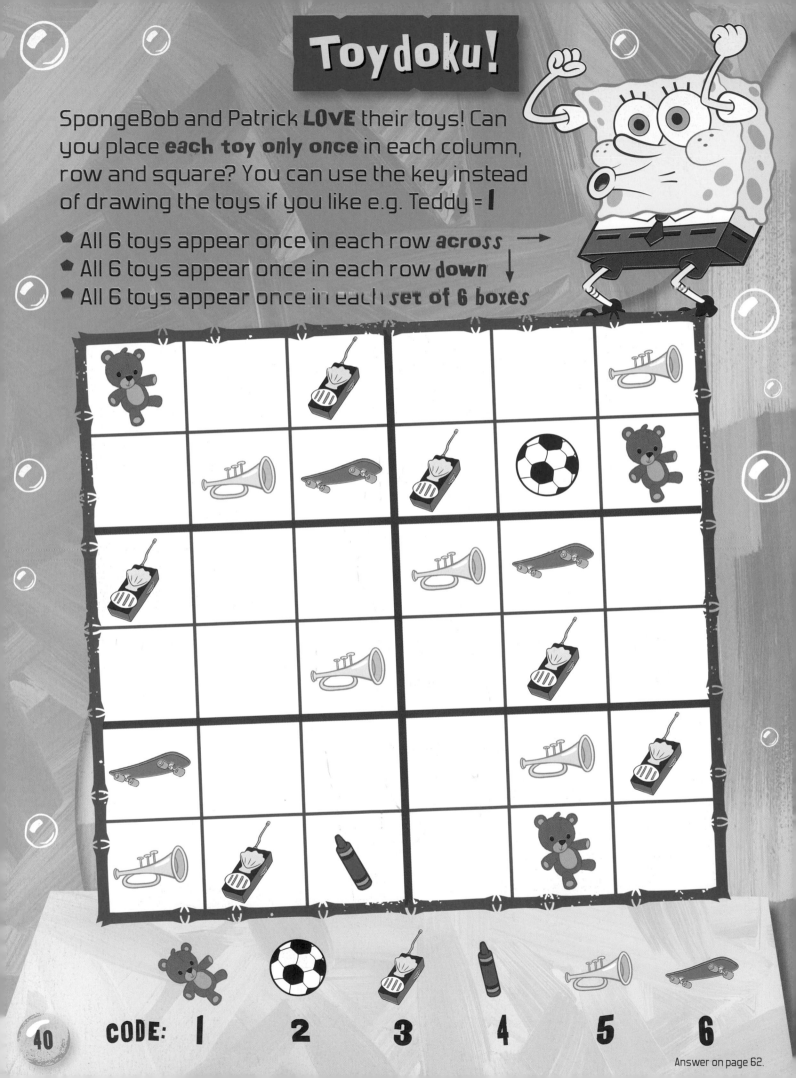

CODE: **1**   **2**   **3**   **4**   **5**   **6**

Answer on page 62.

# Jellyfishing!

**Patrick** and **SpongeBob** are having fun at the Jellyfish Fields. Colour them in!

How many jellyfish can you count on this page?

Answer on page 62.

# That's no Lady!

Add **any words you** like to this
Bikini Bottom adventure!

Based on
one of your
Top 10
Fan Favourites
episodes!

Patrick was **innocently minding** his own business

when he bumped into a strange _____ who gave

him a flyer and told him to **"Get out of town!"**

Patrick was frightened. Why did he have to get out of town?!

He grabbed his _____ and started to pack.

Luckily, SpongeBob came over at that moment to see what

the matter was. Patrick explained. SpongeBob thought for

a second then came up with an _____ plan.

They decided that if Patrick had to get out of town, he

should **become someone else!** He dressed up in a

_____ and a _____ and became Patricia.

SpongeBob took 'Patricia' to work at the _____ and

introduced her to Squidward and Krabs. The plan worked,

**no one had a clue** who 'she' was! In fact Squidward

and Krabs became rather attached to Patricia.

_____ was **confused**. He couldn't understand why Squidward and Krabs were being so nice to him.

Suddenly, he realised. They were **in love with Patricia!** "_____" said Patrick. He'd rather leave town than put up with all that mushy stuff from those two.

Just then, the door to the _____ swung open, and in walked the **strange man** from earlier that day. "Get out of town!" he cried.

SpongeBob had had enough. He demanded to know what was going on. The man gave _____ a flyer. He was promoting his new **holiday service!**

Patrick was relieved and turned back into his old self, leaving Squidward and Krabs feeling _____ .

**The End**

43

# Disguise Time!

Patrick thinks he's being **forced out** of Bikini Bottom, so he dresses up as his ravishing alter ego **Patricia!** Can you spot which other inhabitants of Bikini Bott om are *in disguise* below?

| SPONGehob | Sandy | Scwwrd | mistercrabs |

### Pick your disguise!

Need a disguise, quick? Use this fool-proof method to choose the disguise for you! What to do: Hover your finger over the **top list** and let your finger fall. Then do the same over the **bottom list. Ta da!**

| Giant | Tiny | Purple |
| Angry | Spotted | Stripy |
| Old aged | Magnificent | |

| Bulldog | Fairy | Shire horse |
| Penguin | Baby | Krabby Patty |
| Octopus | | Pineapple |

44

Answers on page 62.

**Guide Patricia** through Bikini Bottom. Make sure you don't bump into Squidward or Mr Krabs on the way! They think Patricia is **beautiful!**

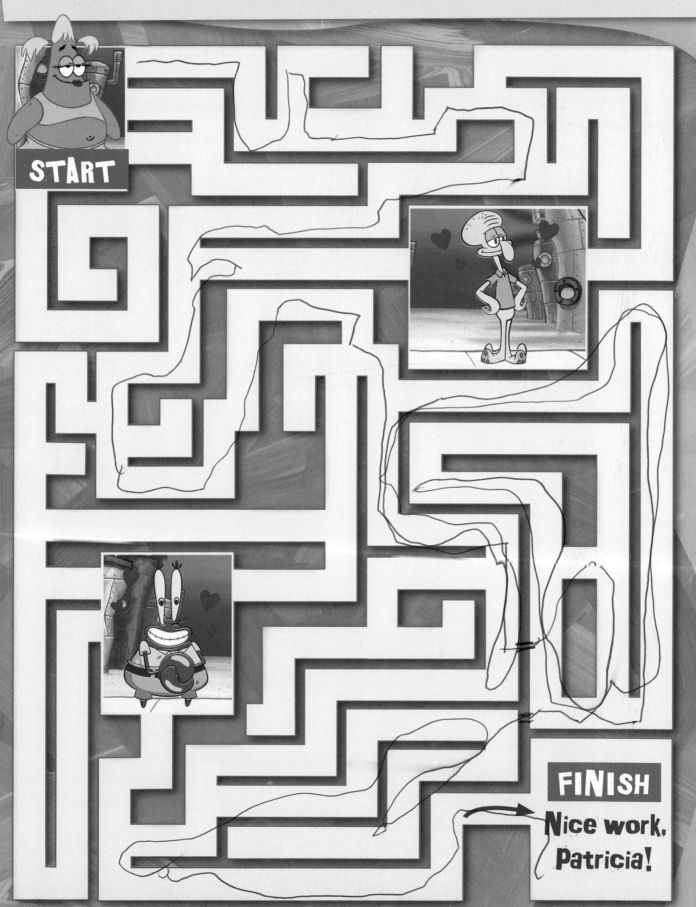

START

FINISH
Nice work, Patricia!

Answer on page 62.

# Dangers of the Deep!

Before you dip a toe into the water, get clued up on our **top 10** fearsome creatures! Spongebob and Patrick are trying their best to be brave!

## 1. Box Jellyfish

It might look like something you could jump up and down on at a birthday party, but this jellyfish has some of the most poisonous venom of any creature in the world!

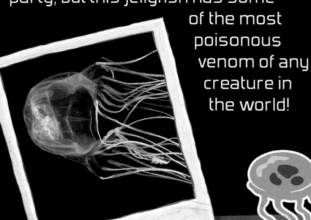

## 2. Great White Shark

These giant man-eaters can detect a single drop of blood in 100 litres of water up to three miles away. **Gulp!**

## 3. Giant Cuttlefish

This freaky-looking fish knows how to defend itself in a fight. It sprays toxic, black ink to blind whatever wants to eat it, then runs away!

## 4. Giant Squid

These mysterious creatures are rarely seen by humans, but can grow to 10 metres long and have eyes the size of beach balls!

## 5. Barracuda

These fish have sharp teeth and are nicknamed the 'Tigers of the Sea'. They might look harmless, but they have a nasty bite!

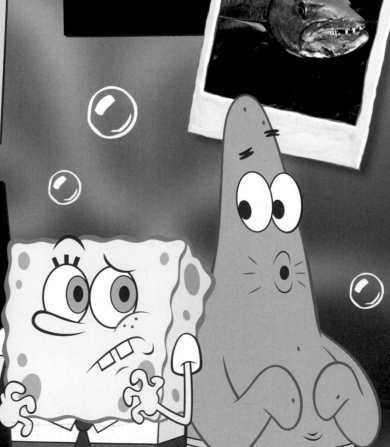

## 6. Giant Octopus

Although they are smaller than their Squiddy cousins, the giant octopus is sneakier. It can change its colour to blend into its habitat and sneak up on prey!

Growing up to the size of a bus and hunting in groups, called pods, these mammals are a scary sight . . . and not just to the seals they hunt!

## 7. Crown of Thorns Starfish

This spiky creature is covered in poisonous thorns that are really painful to stand on and it's pretty dangerous, too!

## 9. Beaded Sea Snake

This snake's venom is one of the most powerful poisons in the world. Luckily they don't often attack humans!

As well as being a scary-looking creature, the Stonefish is the most venomous fish in the world!

**Argh!** Why not try designing your own deep sea monster? Use the terrifying sea creatures to give you some ideas!

# How to draw Plankton!

Use the blank space to **copy Plankton** square-by-square.

**Which Sandy?**

One of these Sandys is an *imposter*! Can you find her?

**a**  **b**  **c**

Answer on page 62.

# F.U.N.

One of your Top 10 Fan Favourites episodes!

**SpongeBob says:**

"It was just another **blissful day** working in the Krusty Krab, frying off my delicious burgers when Sheldon Plankton staged another of his attempts to **steal the secret recipe!** Naturally it was down to yours truly to stop him and get the patty back, but when I finally did, I realised something. Plankton just **needed a friend!** And that friend was going to be me!

The first thing I needed to do was teach Plankton all about having **F.U.N.!** The trouble was, I got the distinct impression all Plankton wanted to do was a spot of **evil plotting**. I decided to be his friend anyway and took him to the Krusty Krab to show off our friendship.

Krabs was certain Plankton was just **using me** to get to the burgers, and he even left one out for Plankton to steal! But nothing happened, so me and my **new BFF** went to the cinema. It was there, dear reader, that my friendship with Plankton ended. I discovered **he HAD** taken the Krabby Patty after all! Guess that's what you get for making friends with a madman!"

**Plankton says:**

"I almost had my hands on that infuriating Krabby Patty when that **stupid yellow sponge** got in my way! I was busy planning my next attack when that same **moron** turned up at my door bleating on about how he wanted to be my friend! **Ha!** Like I need a friend. Well, actually it would be nice ...

Anyway, I decided to use my friendship with SpongeBob to **steal** the Krabby Patty recipe. It was going so well until Krabs got in the way. The **weird square guy** was pretty upset that I had used him, but what do you expect? It's **so much FUN** being me!"

# Burger Bites!

Make these **super-healthy burgers** to keep your own **hunger monster** at bay!

## Ingredients:

1 small onion, chopped and cooked

2 crushed garlic cloves

2 carrots chopped and cooked

1 small butternut squash chopped and cooked

1 small courgette chopped and cooked

100g (4 oz) porridge oats

30g (1 oz) grated Cheddar cheese

1 egg, beaten

Some plain flour

## How to make the burgers:

**1.** Put all the ingredients aside from the flour into a large mixing bowl and use your hands to squidge it all together.

**2.** Clean and dry your hands and dust them with a little flour. Take handfuls of the mixture and roll them into balls. Flatten them into a patty shape and put them on a plate, dusted with flour.

**3.** Once your burgers are made, ask an adult to cook them in a frying pan for 5 mins on each side.

**4.** Pop the cooked patties in a bun with some salad and a slice of cheddar cheese if you like. Enjoy!

**You will need:**

Mixing bowl

Plate

Your hands

An adult

# Design your own Popcorn!

It's **movie night** in SpongeBob's pineapple, and even sea sponges know you can **only eat one treat** while watching the big screen – **POPCORN!** Colour in this popcorn tub, then **mix and match** to create your own **amazing** or **revolting** flavour!

My **POPCORN** flavour is:
salt and sweet
caramel Banana
chees Peanut

**MENU**
- ✓ Salt
- ✓ Peanut butter
- Vinegar
- ✓ Caramel
- Onion
- ✓ Cheese
- ✓ Banana
- Spinach
- ✓ Seaweed

Which film would **YOU** go and see with SpongeBob?

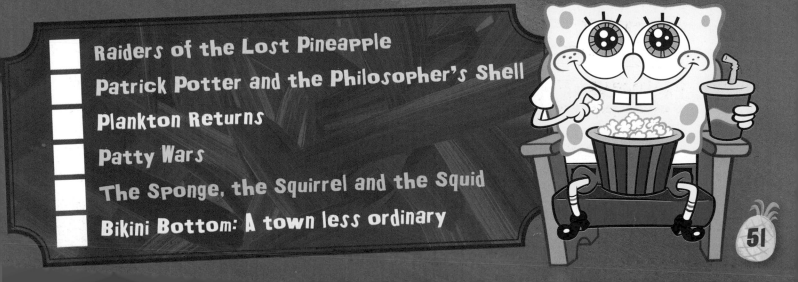

- Raiders of the Lost Pineapple
- Patrick Potter and the Philosopher's Shell
- Plankton Returns
- Patty Wars
- The Sponge, the Squirrel and the Squid
- Bikini Bottom: A town less ordinary

# Puzzles

Get to the bottom of this word ladder by changing **one letter at a time!**

*Less is more!*

L E S S

_ O _ _

_ _ _ E

_ _ V _

_ _ _ _

M O R E

## Patrick's Packed Search

Patrick is off **jellyfishing**, and he's remembered the most important thing of all – no, not a net! **Food!**

Can you find Patrick's picnic essentials in the grid?

KELPO      ICE

FRIES      CREAM

BURGER     BON BONS

| B | U | R | G | E | R |
|---|---|---|---|---|---|
| O | S | E | I | R | F |
| N | F | G | H | M | X |
| B | C | V | B | A | N |
| O | O | P | L | E | K |
| N | X | C | V | R | R |
| S | I | C | E | C | B |

# Order Up!

Can you finish these customer's orders by **completing the sequences?**

Which bit is the one **missing** from the picture?

**a**

**b**

**53**

# Idiot Box

One of your **Top 10** Fan Favourites episodes!

Patrick and SpongeBob were waiting for the postman. They were getting something **very exciting** delivered. "Our package!" squealed SpongeBob.

It was a **giant screen TV!** But SpongeBob and Patrick weren't interested in that. They just wanted **the box**.

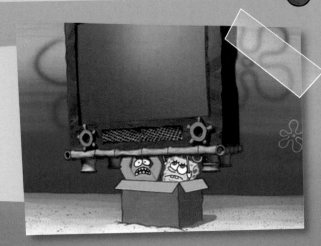

"Hey, **can I have your TV?**" asked Squidward.

"Sure Squidward. Who needs TV when you've got imagin-aaaation?!"

So, Squidward settled down to watch his new TV, but he was soon disturbed by SpongeBob and Patrick playing **Mountain Climbing Adventure!** It sounded like they were in the middle of an **avalanche**, but when Squidward opened the box, there was **nothing inside it ...**

"How did you do that?" he asked.

"With the **power of our imaginations!**" replied SpongeBob.

All night, SpongeBob and Patrick played more and more exciting games in the box. They sounded **so real**, that Squidward was sure something funny was going on. He waited until everything went quiet, then **snuck out** to play in the box.

"There **must be a button** in here somewhere, no one can have that much fun with their imaginations and a box!" he said. Just then, the **box began to move!** "It's working!" Squidward cried.

But Squidward **hadn't** got the box to move at all! It had been **picked up** by the rubbish men!

**The End**

# Box Love

## How many **boxes** can you **count**?

There are

_____

boxes

P.S.
SpongeBob doesn't count!

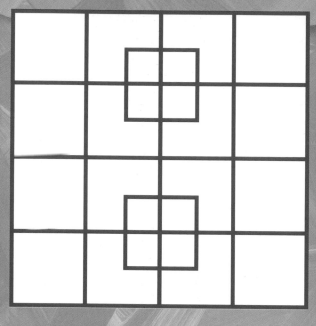

# Angry Squidward

Squidward can't stand not having an imagination like SpongeBob and Patrick's! Which shadow matches this picture of the **grumpiest squid** this side of Bikini Bottom?

**56**

# Imagination Box

SpongeBob and Patrick used *their imaginations* to create whole worlds *inside their box*. What **world** would you **create** in yours? Have a go here!

# Band Geeks

Add **any words you** like to this
Bikini Bottom adventure!

Based on one of your Top 10 Fan Favourites episodes!

Squidward was practicing his **clarinet**, when his

shellphone _____. It was the _____

**Squilliam Fancyson!** He asked Squidward if his band

could fill in for him at a gig at the Bubble Bowl. Squidward

_____. He didn't have a band, but there was

**NO WAY** he was going to admit that to Squilliam!

Squidward **needed a band** fast! He put up _____

all over town and soon he had a group ready to start

making music. Unfortunately, they were all _____.

But that wasn't going to stop Squidward. He made his new

group **practice and practice**, but they were still

_____. In the end, he gave up hope.

It was down to SpongeBob to get **everyone in shape**.

When the day of the _____ finally arrived,

everyone was really nervous.

Squidward was ready to **admit defeat** to Squilliam, but then his band turned up and they were **amazing**! SpongeBob was on _____ , Patrick played the _____ and Mr Krabs was on the keyboard. Even _____ joined in! Squilliam was **so shocked** at their success that he _____ !

The End

## Mixed up Music!

Unscramble these letters to find the **instruments!**

PINAO _____

VIIOLN _____

DURMS _____

# Band Call!

Squidward has called his band together for a rehearsal, but he **can't find** SpongeBob, Patrick or his clarinet. Can **you**?

Answers on page 62.

How many fish are there in the band **altogether**?

Oh, no! SpongeBob dropped his Krabby Patty! Can you track it down, so Plankton can't steal it!

What would **you** call **your** band? Why not design your band's **logo** here?

# Pitch Perfect

Patrick has **lost** some of Squidward's sheet music! Can you tell **which note** should **come next** in each sequence? Quick, before Squidward realises!

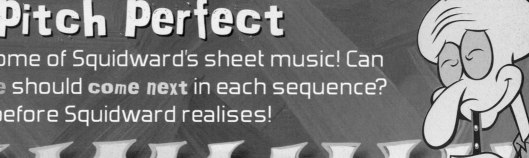

**a**

*Write the next note in the sequence here!*

**b**

**c**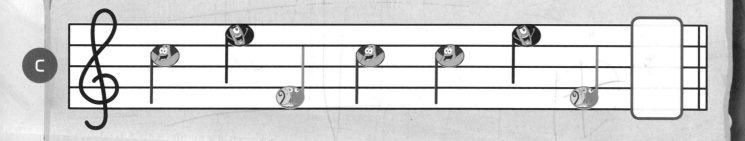

**d**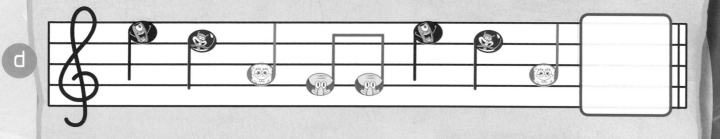

**e**

61

Answers on page 62.

# Answers

## P.08 – Welcome to Bikini Bottom
Larry the Lobster is in front of Sandy's dome. Barnacleboy is waiting to go into the Krusty Krab. The Mayor of Bikini Bottom is next to Squidward's house.

## P.11 – Patrick Star's Top 10 facts
There are 8 jellyfish on the page.

## P.22 – Sink or Swim
Ice cubes – float; Plastic bottle – float; Apple – float; Teacup – sink; Bunch of keys – sink; Mobile phone – sink.

## P.23 – Spot the Difference!
There is a fish at the porthole; The time on the clock has changed; The green crayon is missing; Mrs Puff's bow has become purple; Patrick's glasses are missing.

## P.28 – How Many Krabby Patties?
There are 14 Krabby Patties. Plankton is hidden at the bottom right of the picture, licking a Krabby Patty. Eurgh!

## P.29 – Krusty Wordsearch

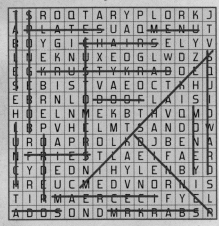

The missing word is Krabby Patties – Plankton must have stolen it for secret tests!

## P.30 – Form an orderly queue ...
FRIES; SODA; PATTIES; MILKSHAKE.

## P.31 – Underwater Wordgrid

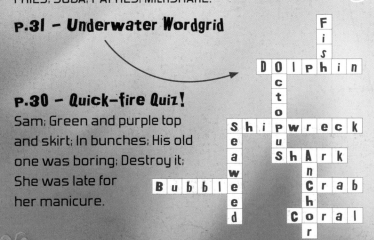

## P.30 – Quick-fire Quiz!
Sam; Green and purple top and skirt; In bunches; His old one was boring; Destroy it; She was late for her manicure.

## P.40 – Toydoku

## P.41 – Jellyfishing!
There are 11 jellyfish on the page. That's about 7 jars of Jellyfish Jam. Yummy!

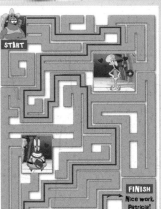

## P.44 – Disguise Time!
In disguise (from left to right) are: SpongeBob, Sandy, Squidward and Mr Krabs

## P.48 – Which Sandy?
C is the imposter. She is missing the red dot on her boot.

## P.52 – Puzzles
LESS, LOSS, LOSE, LOVE, MOVE, MORE.

## P.53 – Order Up!
Ketchup; Burger; Drink. Piece a completes the puzzle.

## P.56 – Box Love
There are 40 boxes in total in the image. Shadow b matches Angry Squidward.

## P.59 – Mixed up Music!
TRUMPET; PIANO; VIOLIN; DRUMS.

## P.60 – Band Call!

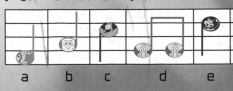

There are 13 fish in the band altogether.

## P.61 – Pitch Perfect

a    b    c    d    e

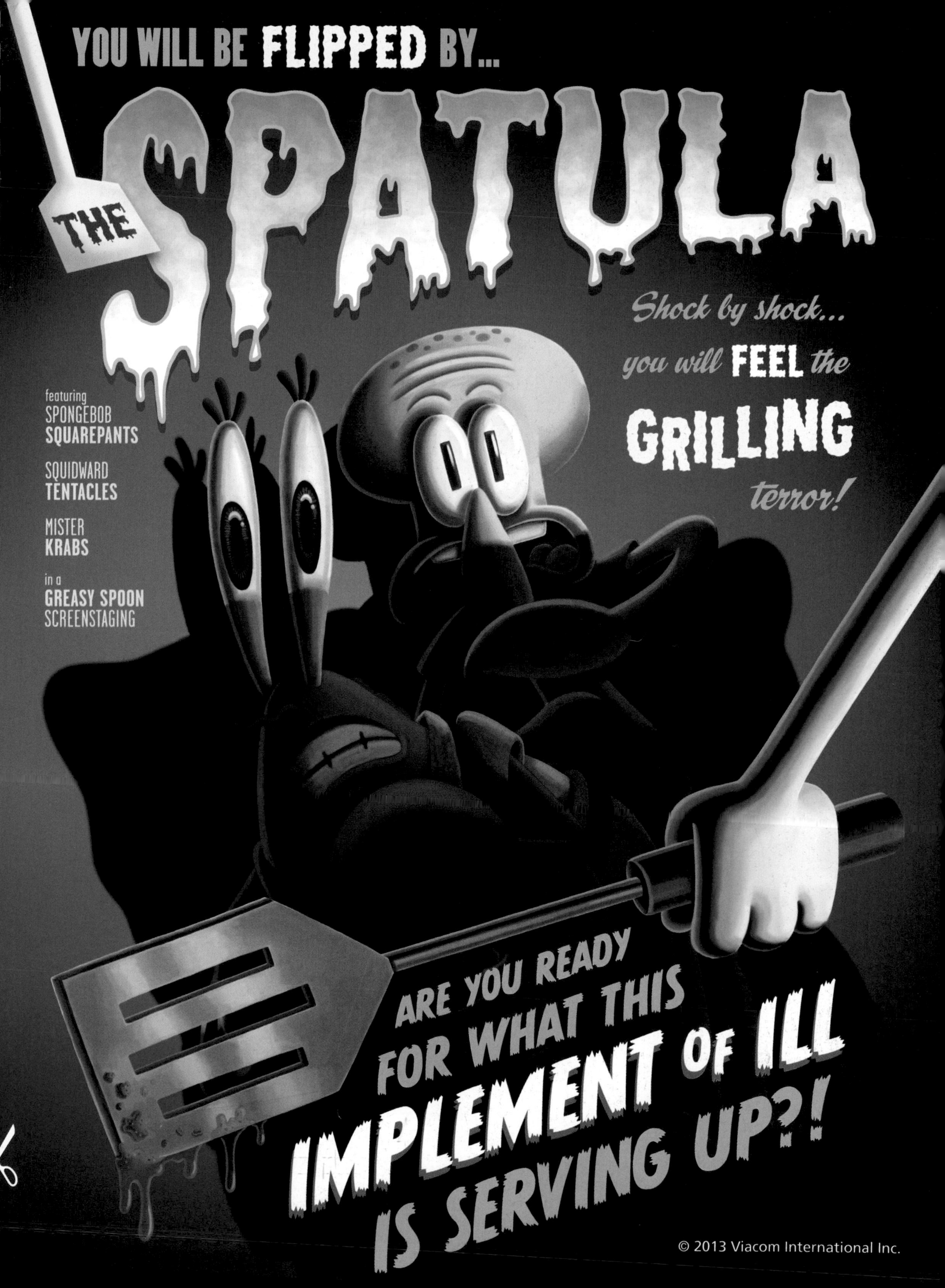


© 2013 Viacom International Inc.

© 2013 Viacom International Inc.

© 2013 Viacom International Inc.

# Reader Survey

We'd love to know what you think about your SpongeBob SquarePants Annual.

Ask a grown-up to help you fill in this form and post it to the address at the end by 28th February 2014, or you can fill in the survey online at:

www.egmont.co.uk/spongebobsurvey2014

**ONE LUCKY READER WILL WIN £150 OF BOOK TOKENS!**

**FIVE RUNNERS-UP WILL WIN A £25 BOOK TOKEN EACH.**

## 1. Who bought this annual?
- ☐ Me
- ☐ Parent/guardian
- ☐ Grandparent
- ☐ Other (please specify)

_____

## 2. Why did they buy it?
- ☐ Christmas present
- ☐ Birthday present
- ☐ I'm a collector
- ☐ Other (please specify)

_____

## 3. What are your favourite parts of the annual?

| | | | |
|---|---|---|---|
| Stories | ☐ Really like | ☐ Like | ☐ Don't like |
| Puzzles and quizzes | ☐ Really like | ☐ Like | ☐ Don't like |
| Colouring | ☐ Really like | ☐ Like | ☐ Don't like |
| Character profiles | ☐ Really like | ☐ Like | ☐ Don't like |
| Posters | ☐ Really like | ☐ Like | ☐ Don't like |
| Facts | ☐ Really like | ☐ Like | ☐ Don't like |
| Things to make | ☐ Really like | ☐ Like | ☐ Don't like |

## 4. Do you think the stories are too long, too short or about right?
- ☐ Too long
- ☐ Too short
- ☐ About right

## 5. Do you think the activities are too hard, too easy or about right?
- ☐ Too hard
- ☐ Too easy
- ☐ About right

## 6. Who are your favourite characters?

1. _____
2. _____
3. _____

## 7. Which other annuals do you like?

1. _____
2. _____
3. _____

## 8. What is your favourite ...

1. ... app or website? _____
2. ... console game? _____
3. ... magazine? _____
4. ... book? _____

## 9. What are your favourite TV programmes?

1. _____
2. _____
3. _____

## 10. Would you like to get this annual again next year?

☐ Yes
☐ No
Why? _____
_____

## Thank you!

Child's name: _____ Age: _____ Boy/Girl

Parent/guardian name: _____

Parent/guardian signature: _____

Parent/guardian email address: _____

Daytime telephone number: _____

☐ Please send me the Egmont Monthly Catch-Up Newsletter.

Please cut out and post to: SpongeBob SquarePants Annual Reader Survey, Egmont UK Limited, The Yellow Building, 1 Nicholas Road, London, W11 4AN

Good luck!

Promoter: Egmont UK Limited ("Egmont"). The Competition will be open for entries until the end of 28th February 2014 (the "Closing Date"). Any entries received after of the Closing Date will be invalid. The Competition is open to permanent UK residents only. The Competition is not open to employees of Egmont or their immediate families. Entry is free of charge – no purchase is necessary. You may enter the Competition by post or you can enter online at www.egmont.co.uk/spongebobsurvey2014. No more than one entry per entrant. No responsibility can be accepted for entries that are lost or delayed or that are not received for any reason. There is one prize of £150 of book tokens and five runners up prizes of £25 book tokens to be won. The winner will be drawn at random from all the entries received by the Closing Date. If you are the winner, you will be notified by email or phone no later than 28 days after the Closing Date. If you want to know who wins, please send a stamped, addressed envelope to us marking clearly that you want to know about the Annuals Competition. We will give you the winner's first name and county only. Please note that further terms and conditions apply: see www.egmont.co.uk/competitionterms.

ADVERTISEMENT